ANIMAL PREDATORS

Owls

SANDRA MARKLE

LERNER BOOKS • LONDON • NEW YORK • MINNEAPOLIS

THE ANIMAL WORLD IS FULL OF
PREDATORS.

Predators are the hunters who find, catch and eat other animals — their prey — in order to survive. Every environment has its chain of hunters. The smaller, slower, less able predators become prey for the bigger, faster, more cunning hunters. Everywhere, there are just a few kinds of predators at the top of the food chain.

In nearly every habitat, this group of predators includes one or more kinds of owls, like this screech owl.

So why are owls, like this great grey owl, such great hunters? First, they can swoop through the air almost silently to strike with their sharp talons (claws) and beak. Secondly, because most owls hunt at night they have bigger eyes than most birds. Their big eyes face forwards so they can judge how far to fly to catch their prey. Their eyes also have powerful magnifying lenses so they can spot small prey from long distances. The pupils of their eyes (the openings at the centre) can open very wide to let in more light when it is dark.

For protection and support, an owl's big eyes are inside bony tubes. These tubes limit how much its eyes can move. To look left, right, up or down, owls — like this northern saw-whet — must turn their heads. All owls' necks have lots of bones — nearly twice as many as a human's neck. These bones let the owl turn its head far enough to look almost straight behind itself.

This barn owl's disc-shaped face collects sound waves in the same way that a satellite dish collects radio waves. Under the feathers are huge ear openings. One is usually larger and lower on the owl's head than the other. This difference in size and position helps the owl quickly work out where sounds are coming from.

The female great grey's feathers blend perfectly with the tree bark. While she rests, her big yellow eyes are half-closed and hidden by feathery lids. Then she hears a gopher's (an American rodent) rustling noise. Her eyes snap wide open and she studies the shadowy ground.

The instant a gopher runs into the open, the great grey owl launches into flight. The great grey is among the world's biggest owls. The female's body is about 80 centimetres tall, and her wings stretch nearly 1.5 metres from tip to tip. Her large size makes her a powerful predator. She is able to kill bigger prey, such as rabbits and squirrels, that smaller owls couldn't catch. Her large size also means that she needs more energy to fly, so the great grey prefers to hunt by perching and waiting. When prey comes within range, she drops off the branch, spreads her wings to slow her plunge, and swoops down.

This time, the big owl will need to fly a short distance to overtake her prey. She does this almost silently. The front edges of most birds' wings are solid, like stiff fingers pressed together. Such wings smack against the air with a thump. Whereas the leading edges of an owl's wings are fringed and flexible, like rubbery fingers spread apart. The upper surface of each feather also has a velvet coat of tiny strands. The great grey's wings slip through the air with the softest swish. When the female great grey is nearly over the gopher, she pulls in her wings and dives to attack.

The owl's fourth toe is turned backwards to work like a thumb. She grabs the gopher with one foot.

Next, the great grey uses another weapon — her sharp beak. A bristly feather moustache around her beak lets her feel when she's close enough to bite her prey. Then she quickly kills it.

The great grey's wings provide enough lifting power to fly while carrying prey, allowing her to fly back to her favourite perch. High above the forest floor, she can eat, safe from ground-hunting predators like foxes, who might try to steal her meal. No longer out in the open, she is also less likely to have to defend her food from flying predators, such as hawks and other owls.

Like this pygmy owl, all owls have wide mouths. Whenever possible they swallow their prey in one gulp. If the meal is really big, the owl will rip off chunks.

Next, digestive juices in the owl's stomach go to work. The digestive juices can't break down the prey's teeth, fur or bones. The food passes from the stomach into a muscular sac called the gizzard. There, the broken-down food is turned into a soft mass and passed on into the intestine to finish being digested.

The bits left in the gizzard are squeezed and packed together to form a soft pellet. This pellet is then regurgitated by the owl. If an owl perches in the same spot every day, the forest floor below becomes littered with these pellets.

An owl needs to fly in order to catch food. So when it isn't flying the owl spends a lot of time preening or caring for its feathers. This burrowing owl carefully pulls each of its outer feathers through its beak.

Feathers are made up of hundreds of strands held together by tiny hooks. Flying or struggling with prey can separate the feather strands. All owls, including this screech owl, have to preen regularly to fasten their feathers together again.

The feathers of an owl's coat often match its surroundings. This helps it to hide wherever it is waiting to ambush (surprise) its prey. The Arctic region has few trees and a lot of snow much of the year. The snowy owl's colouring camouflages (hides) it when it is sitting on the ground in the Arctic.

This male snowy owl was waiting next to the entrance to a lemming's tunnel. When the lemming started running, the snowy owl was only a hop away. He'll deliver this meal to his mate.

This male barn owl is delivering a meal too. It's a gift to win a mate. Most owls start nesting in late winter. The female will need to spend about a month sitting on her eggs. This will keep them warm while the babies grow inside the eggs. The male's food gift shows he can be counted on to do all of the hunting during this time.

Whoo, hoo-hoo-hoo. Whoo, hoo-hoo-hoo. This male great horned owl flies from perch to perch. At each stop, he hoots loudly to tell other great horned males to stay away from his territory. This territory is often a large area, where he will hunt to feed his mate and offspring (young).

Female owls lay their eggs as long as four days apart. The first chicks to hatch may be two weeks older than the youngest ones. At first, the chicks' eyes are closed and their feathers are thin. This mother great grey owl keeps the chicks close to her warm body. When it rains, she holds her wings open over them like a feathery umbrella.

When a hawk circles overhead, looking for a meal, the mother great grey owl fluffs up her feathers to make herself look bigger. When the hawk swoops closer, the mother owl hisses and clicks her beak noisily. This threat works and the hawk flies away. While the mother owl stays with her young family, the father owl keeps on hunting.

At first, owl chicks or owlets are too small to swallow prey whole. The female screech owl tears off small, boneless bits of meat from the prey the male has brought her. Then, closing her eyes to protect them from the chick's beak, she feeds the bits to her offspring. This food is easier for the chick to eat because it doesn't contain any bones or fur that it could possibly choke on.

When the chick is full, it goes back into its nest. This nest is a natural hole in the tree. Most owls don't build nests, but sometimes they take over the abandoned nest of a hawk or a crow. More often, they find a hole in a tree or use a broken treetop for a nest. Owls don't even add any nesting material. The eggs and the young rest directly on the wood chips and other matter that are already on the floor of the hole.

The female snowy owl's nest is just a dip in the ground. Like the screech owl, the mother snowy owl tears off bits of meat for her babies. She starts by feeding the chicks that are begging most actively. These are usually the older, bigger chicks. So if the meal isn't very big, the smaller chicks get less to eat. If food becomes scarce, the younger chicks may die. They may even become food for the older chicks. That way, at least some of the owlets survive.

This tawny owl is delivering a rabbit to the chicks. Male owls spend a lot of time and energy hunting to provide food for the growing owlets.

Eventually, growing owlets get so big that both parents must hunt to keep their hungry offspring fed. Left on their own, these young screech owls huddle together to keep warm and safe. Side by side, the three little owlets look much bigger and are less likely to be attacked by any hungry hawks or other owls flying overhead.

The wings of these ten-week-old horned owls are not yet strong enough for flight. That doesn't stop the owlets from exploring by walking along the branches. When one owlet starts to fall, he grabs onto the branch with his talons. Then he uses his beak to pull himself up onto the branch again.

This young screech owl is strong and practised enough to fly, but its hunting skills are weak. With practice, the youngster quickly learns to catch easy prey, like this hawkmoth caterpillar.

When this young female saw-whet owl first tried to catch a mouse, the mouse escaped. Hunger forced the young female to keep practising. Like all owls, the young saw-whet was naturally equipped to be a good hunter. Her colouring acts as a camouflage, allowing her to hide unseen while she watches for prey. Her excellent hearing and eyesight let her detect and pinpoint prey even in poor light. Her fringed feathers let her fly almost silently to surprise her prey. The young owl only has to perfect the timing of her attack.

Finally, the female saw-whet is successful. As she grabs the mouse, the young owl becomes part of a new generation of hunters on the wing.

With love for good friends Terry and Kath Mundy

The author would like to thank Irina Menyushina, research scientist for Wrangel Island State Nature Reserve, Russia, for sharing her expertise and enthusiasm, and especially for her many years studying snowy owls in the wild. And a very special thanks to Skip Jeffery for his help and support.

First published in the United Kingdom in 2008 by
Lerner Books,
Dalton House,
60 Windsor Avenue,
London SW19 2RR

Website address: www.lernerbooks.co.uk

This edition was updated and edited for UK publication by Discovery Books Ltd.,
Unit 3, 37 Watling Street, Leintwardine, Shropshire SY7 0LW

British Library Cataloguing in Publication Data

Markle, Sandra
  Owls. - (Animal predators)
  1. Owls - Juvenile literature
  I. Title
  598.9'7

ISBN-13: 978 1 58013 415 6

Photo Acknowledgements

The images in this book are used with the permission of: © Lanz Von Horsten/ABPL/Animals Animals, p. 1; © Joe McDonald/CORBIS, pp. 3, 20, 33, 35; © Erwin & Peggy Bauer/Wildstock, pp. 4, 7; © Maslowski Productions, pp. 5, 8, 21, 22, 23, 24, 28, 31; © W. Perry Conway/CORBIS, p. 6; © Daniel J. Cox/NaturalExposures.com, p. 11; © Michael Quinton, pp. 12, 14, 27, 34; © Joe McDonald/Bruce Coleman, Inc., p. 13; © Claus Meyer/Minden Pictures, p. 17; © John Hoffman/Bruce Coleman, Inc., p. 18; © Phyllis Greenberg/Animals Animals, p. 19; © Gary R. Jones/Bruce Coleman, Inc., p. 26; © Andy Harmer, p. 32; © Dwight R. Kuhn, p. 36.

Front Cover: © Stephen Dalton/Animals Animals.